MATH MASTERS ANALYZE THIS!

Factors and Multiples

Melanie Alvarez

Rourke
Educational Media

rourkeeducationalmedia.com

Before Reading:

Building Academic Vocabulary and Background Knowledge

Before reading a book, it is important to tap into what your child or students already know about the topic. This will help them develop their vocabulary, increase their reading comprehension, and make connections across the curriculum.

1. *Look at the cover of the book. What will this book be about?*
2. *What do you already know about the topic?*
3. *Let's study the Table of Contents. What will you learn about in the book's chapters?*
4. *What would you like to learn about this topic? Do you think you might learn about it from this book? Why or why not?*
5. *Use a reading journal to write about your knowledge of this topic. Record what you already know about the topic and what you hope to learn about the topic.*
6. *Read the book.*
7. *In your reading journal, record what you learned about the topic and your response to the book.*
8. *After reading the book complete the activities below.*

Content Area Vocabulary

Read the list. What do thes words mean?

basic facts
cicadas
contributed
divisible
infinite
inverse operation
numerical
previous
prime factorization
ratios

After Reading:

Comprehension and Extension Activity

After reading the book, work on the following questions with your child or students in order to c their level of reading comprehension and content mastery.

1. *Name two ways you can write a number's factors.* (Summarize)
2. *How long do multiples go on for?* (Infer)
3. *How do you find common multiples of two or more numbers?* (Asking questions)
4. *Explain what a common factor is.* (Text to self connection)
5. *What does LCM stand for?* (Asking questions)

Extension Activity

Practice all the concepts in the book to master factors and multiples!

Table of Contents

What are Factors?

Factors are numbers that are multiplied to get other numbers.

FACTOR x FACTOR = PRODUCT

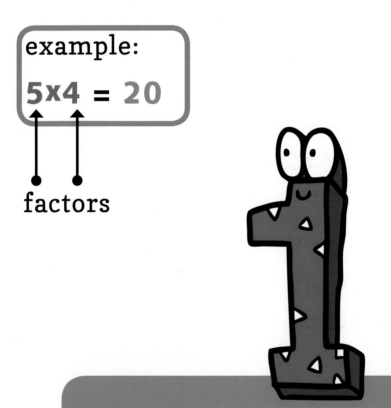

example:

5x4 = 20

factors

The Identity Property of Multiplication (sometimes called the Multiplication Property of One) says that a number does not change if it is multiplied by 1. This means that even a number as large as 10 million multiplied by 1 will be itself: 10 million.

The factors of 20 are the numbers that you can multiply by in order to get 20.

Here are the **basic facts** that have 20 as an answer:

(1) x 20 = 20

(20) x 1 = 20

(2) x 10 = 20

(10) x 2 = 20

(4) x 5 = 20

(5) x 4 = 20

20

All of the numbers that create 20 using multiplication are factors of 20. Look at a multiplication chart to find the factors of 20.

MULTIPLICATION TABLE 1-20

X	1	2	3	4	5	6	7	8	9	10	11	12	13	14	15	16	17	18	19	2
1	1	2	3	4	5	6	7	8	9	10	11	12	13	14	15	16	17	18	19	
2	2	4	6	8	10	12	14	16	18	20	22	24	26	28	30	32	34	36	38	
3	3	6	9	12	15	18	21	24	27	30	33	36	39	42	45	48	51	54	57	
4	4	8	12	16	20	24	28	32	36	40	44	48	52	56	60	64	68	72	76	
5	5	10	15	20	25	30	35	40	45	50	55	60	65	70	75	80	85	90	95	1
6	6	12	18	24	30	36	42	48	54	60	66	72	78	84	90	96	102	108	114	1
7	7	14	21	28	35	42	49	56	63	70	77	84	91	98	105	112	119	126	133	1
8	8	16	24	32	40	48	56	64	72	80	88	96	104	112	120	128	136	144	152	1
9	9	18	27	36	45	54	63	72	81	90	99	108	117	126	135	145	153	162	171	1
10	10	20	30	40	50	60	70	80	90	100	110	120	130	140	150	160	170	180	190	2
11	11	22	33	44	55	66	77	88	99	110	121	132	143	154	165	176	187	198	209	2
12	12	24	36	48	60	72	84	96	108	120	132	144	156	168	180	192	204	216	228	2
13	13	26	39	52	65	78	91	104	117	130	143	156	169	182	195	208	221	234	247	2
14	14	28	42	56	70	84	98	112	126	140	154	168	182	196	210	224	238	252	266	2
15	15	30	45	60	75	90	105	120	135	150	165	180	195	210	225	240	255	270	285	3
16	16	32	48	64	80	96	112	128	144	160	176	192	208	224	240	256	272	288	304	3
17	17	34	51	68	85	102	119	136	153	170	187	204	221	238	255	272	289	306	323	3
18	18	36	54	72	90	108	126	144	162	180	198	216	234	252	270	288	306	324	342	3
19	19	38	57	76	95	114	133	152	172	190	209	228	247	266	285	304	323	342	361	3
20	20	40	60	80	100	120	140	160	180	200	220	240	260	280	300	320	340	360	380	4

You can write a number's factors in many ways. Here are a few:

Rainbow Method

Factors of 20: 1, 2, 4, 5, 10, 20

Factor Rainbow for 20

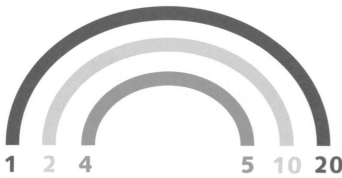

1 2 4   5 10 20

The factor pairs are written down and connected in **numerical** order. You complete all the possible factors when you meet in the middle. Since 4 and 5 are next to each other on the number line, you know you are done writing the factors of 20.

T-Chart for 20

20	
1	20
2	10
4	5

A T-chart sorts factors as pairs. You are done making the T-chart when you have reached an **inverse operation**, like 4 x 5 = 20 and 5 x 4 = 20.

Some whole numbers have only two factors, 1 and themself. These are called prime numbers. Some examples of prime numbers include 1, 2, 3, 5, 7, 11, 13, 17, 19, 23, 29, 31, and 37. There is an **infinite** amount of prime numbers since there is an infinite amount of numbers. In fact, the largest known prime number has around 22 million digits!

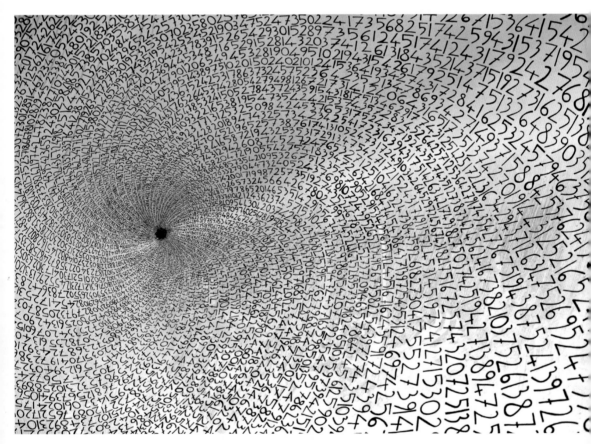

Can you imagine writing a number 22 million digits long? How long do you think the piece of paper would have to be?

Whole numbers that are not prime are called composite numbers. These are numbers that have more factors than just one and themself.

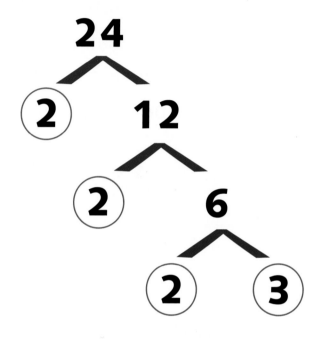

Finding the **prime factorization** of a number requires you to identify the prime numbers that multiply to make the original number. The prime factorization of each positive number is unique. That set of prime numbers cannot make any other number. In a way, prime numbers are the building blocks of all others!

What are Multiples?

Multiples are the products of a counting number and any other counting number. Using the **previous** example of the number 20, you find that the multiples of 20 are all greater than 20. You can find multiples by skip counting. So the multiples of 20 would be 40, 60, 80, 100, 120, and so on.

20

40

60

80

100

120...

Multiples are interesting because they go on forever. This means that each counting number has an infinite number of multiples.

Did you know that insects called **cicadas** spend most of their lives underground? Many species only come above ground every 13th or 17th year. Even cicadas are skip counting to find multiples! Isn't it fascinating how nature and math go together?

Because each number has an infinite number of multiples, when your teacher asks you to list the multiples of 6, make sure
you ask how many you should list. Otherwise, you could be in your classroom listing the multiples of six until you are old and gray!

Here are some examples of multiples.

Multiples of 10: 10, 20, 30, 40, 50, 60, 70, 80…

Multiples of 4: 4, 8, 12, 16, 20, 24, 28, 32…

Multiples of 7: 7, 14, 21, 28, 35, 42, 49, 56…

If you look at these multiples closely, you will see that they are the answers, or products, of the basic multiplication facts. For instance, look at the multiples of four. The first eight multiples are listed, so those are the answers to 4x1, 4x2, 4x3, 4x4, 4x5, 4x6, 4x7, and 4x8.

You try some!

1. What are the first six multiples of 5?

_____

2. What are the first six multiples of 8?

_____

3. What are the first six multiples of 12?

_____

Factors Make Multiples!

Now that you have learned about factors and multiples, here are some tips to remember the differences between them.

Even adults sometimes confuse factors with multiples.

The Greek mathematician Euclid studied prime numbers all the way back in 300 BCE! He **contributed** greatly to our understanding of prime numbers, factorization, and divisors.

EVCLIDES
Philosophus Socraticus
Ex Numismate æreo in Thesauro Christinæ Reginæ Aug.
16.

Factors vs. Multiples

• Factors make multiples.	• Multiples are made of factors.
• Factors are never greater than the number you are finding them for.	• Multiples are infinite, meaning they go on forever.
• When comparing the factors and multiples of 8, for example, factors will be the lesser numbers (Example: 1, 2, 4, and 8).	• When comparing the factors and multiples of 8, for example, multiples will be the greater numbers (Example: 8, 16, 24, 32, 40...).
• Every number is a factor of itself.	• Every number is a multiple of itself.
• Every number has the factor 1.	• Every number is a multiple of 1.
• Every number is a factor of zero.	• Zero is a multiple of every number.

What's in Common?: GCF

Two or more numbers can have factors in common. These are called common factors. For example, the numbers 12 and 15 have the common factors 1 and 3.

When trying to find common factors of two or more numbers, first list all the factors of each number. Then, circle the factors the numbers have in common.

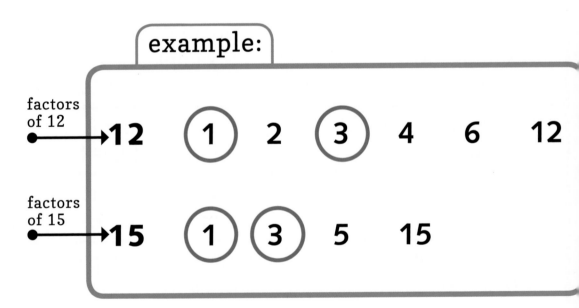

example:

factors of 12

→12 ① 2 ③ 4 6 12

factors of 15

→15 ① ③ 5 15

Can you spot the common factors of the following numbers?

Factors of **8**:   1, 2, 4, 8

Factors of **12**: 1, 2, 3, 4, 6, 12

If you are thinking 1, 2, and 4, then you are correct!

Sometimes you will be asked to find the greatest common factor, or GCF. The GCF is the greatest (largest) of the common factors. To do this, first find the common factors. Then, choose the one that is the greatest of the common factors.

example:

Find the greatest common factor of 24 and 32.

24   (1) (2) 3 (4) 6 (8) 12   24

32   (1) (2) (4) (8) 16   32

Now you try!

1. Find the greatest common factor for 18 and 24.

18 _____

24 _____

2. Find the greatest common factor for 35 and 54.

36 _____

54 _____

3. Find the greatest common factor for 24, 36, 60.

24 _____

36 _____

60 _____

What's in Common?: LCM

Two or more numbers can also have multiples in common. These are called common multiples. For example, the numbers 8 and 5 have the common multiples of 40, 80, 120, 160, and so on. These can be useful when working with fractions and **ratios**.

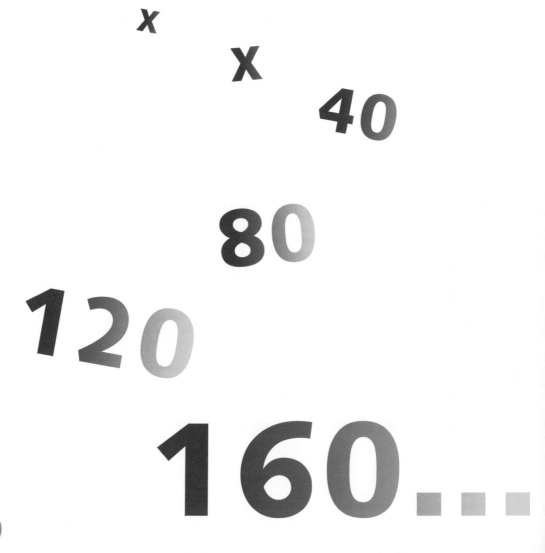

X

X

40

80

120

160...

When trying to find common multiples of two or more numbers, first start listing multiples of each number. Continue until you find some multiples the numbers have in common.

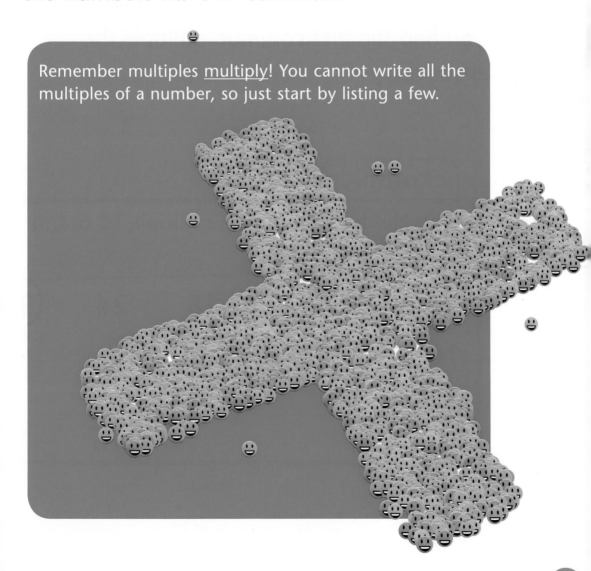

Remember multiples <u>multiply</u>! You cannot write all the multiples of a number, so just start by listing a few.

Sometimes you will be asked to find the least common multiple, or LCM. The LCM is the least (smallest) of the common multiples. It is actually the first common multiple you will come across when listing the multiples of two or more numbers. So, to find the LCM, you simply stop when you find the first common multiple the numbers have.

example:

Find the least common multiple of 6 and 10

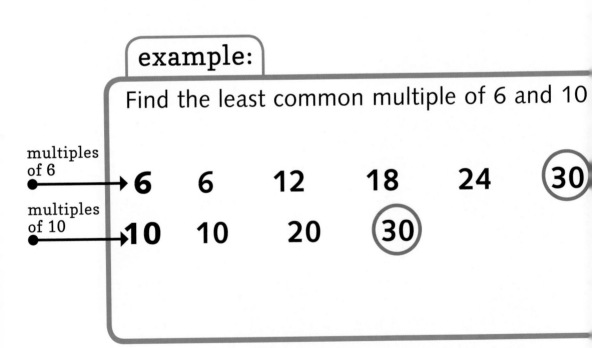

multiples of 6

6   6   12   18   24   30

multiples of 10

10   10   20   30

Now you try!

1. Find the least common multiple of 2 and 5.

2 _____

5 _____

2. Find the least common multiple of 3 and 4.

3 _____

4 _____

3. Find the least common multiple of 4, 12, and 20.

4 _____

12 _____

20 _____

Know Your Facts!

As you can see, in order to fully understand factors and multiples, you need to know the basic facts of multiplication and division pretty well.

One way of doing this is to memorize the three numbers that go together in each basic fact: the two factors and the product.

You can do this by thinking of them as friends who always stick together. Some factors are part of other "friend groups," but when two friends are there, the third always follows.

FACTOR x FACTOR = PRODUCT

Check out these factor friend groups! They like to go to parties together.

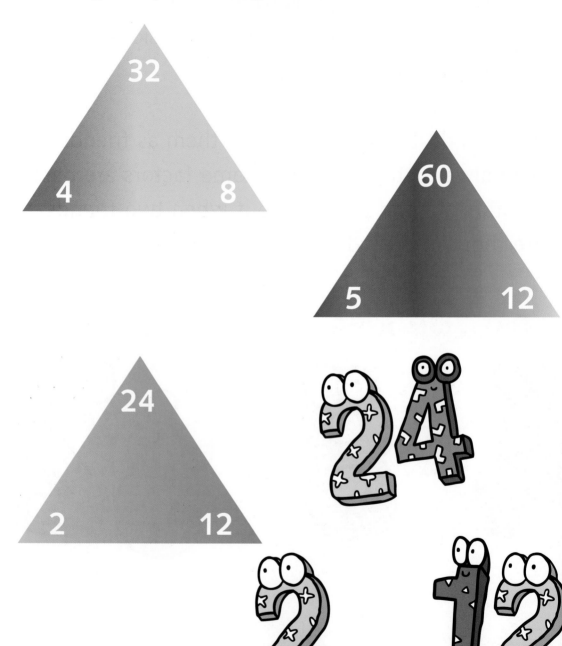

Now you try filling in the missing friends,
or factors, on the triangles.

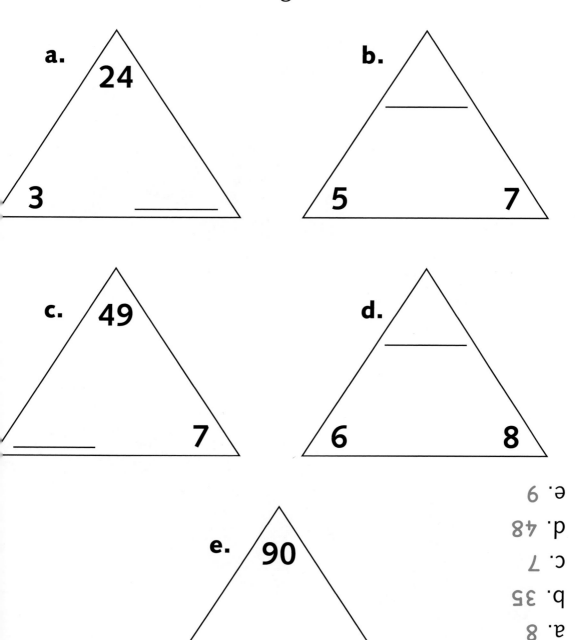

a. 24 / 3 / _____

b. _____ / 5 / 7

c. 49 / _____ / 7

d. _____ / 6 / 8

e. 90 / _____ / 10

For more help with factors and multiples, get to know divisibility rules.

These will help you know which whole numbers other numbers are **divisible** by.

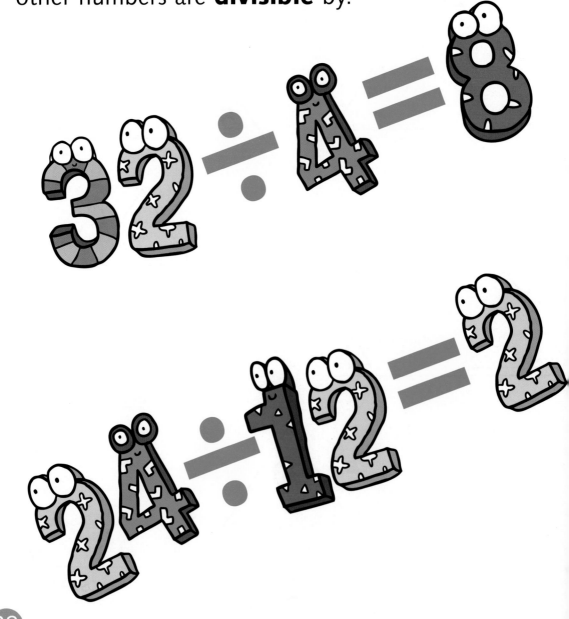

Divisibility Rules

Divisible: able to be divided evenly with no remainder

A number is divisible by ● if...

2 the last digit is even

3 the sum of the digits is divisible by 3

4 the last two digits form a number that is divisible by 4

5 the last digit is a 5 or a 0

6 the number is divisible by both 2 and 3

7 you can double the last digit and subtract the sum from the rest of the number, and set an answer that is divisible by 6 (including 0)

8 the last three digits form a number that is divisible by 8

9 the sum of all the digits is divisible by 9

10 the number ends in 0

Glossary

basic facts (BAY-sik fakts): operations such as addition, subtraction, multiplication, and division performed mainly by using numbers 10 or less

cicadas (si-KAY-dahs): stout-bodied insects that have a wide blunt head, large transparent wings, and the males of which make a loud buzzing noise

contributed (kuhn-TRIB-yoot-ed): to give help to accomplish a specific goal

divisible (di-VIZ-uh-bul): able to be divided

infinite (IN-fuh-nit): too large to be measured or counted

inverse operation (IN-vurs ah-puh-RAY-shuhn): opposite operation

numerical (noo-MER-i-kuhl): related to or expressed with numbers

previous (PREE-vee-uhs): former, or happening before

prime factorization (prime FAK-tur-i-zay-shuhn): the process in which you write a composite number as a product of its prime factors

ratios (RAY-shee-ohs): comparisons of two quantities or numbers using division

Index

Websites to Visit

www.e-learningforkids.org/math/lesson/penguins-factors-
     multiples
www.math-play.com/Factors-and-Multiples-Jeopardy/Factors-
     and-Multiples-Jeopardy.html
nrich.maths.org/5468

About The Author

Melanie M. Alvarez is a sixth grade mathematics teacher at an environmentally focused charter school in Florida. When she is not working as a teacher, private tutor, or writer, she enjoys spending time with her husband and two sons. Melanie is a firm believer in the power of reading and in raising her children and students to be lifelong learners.

Meet The Author!
www.meetREMauthors.com

www.rourkeeducationalmedia.com

PHOTO CREDITS: Cover: numbers © brain/lightbulb © Positive Vectors, Tree © Kalenik Hanna, sky and grass © madams; page 4, 17 and pages 25-26 © Gazoukoo; page 5 stop sign © Becky Stares; page 6 © Sufi; page 8 © Balaz5, page 11 © Yuriy Kulik, page 12 © sundatoon page 14 © ©Welcomeimages.org, page 21 © Jakub Grygier, page 24 © Piyaphat Detbun. All images from Shutterstock.com except page 1

Edited by: Keli Sipperley

Cover and Interior design by: Nicola Stratford   www.nicolastratford.com

Library of Congress PCN Data

Factors and Mulitples / Melanie Alvarez
(Math Masters: Analyze This!)
 ISBN 978-1-68191-736-8 (hard cover)
 ISBN 978-1-68191-837-2 (soft cover)
 ISBN 978-1-68191-930-0 (e-Book)
Library of Congress Control Number: 2016932660

Also Available as:

Rourke Educational Media
Printed in the United States of America, North Mankato, Minnesota